# SOMETIMES A SINGLE LEAF

# ESTHER DISCHEREIT

# SOMETIMES
# A SINGLE LEAF
## SELECTED POEMS

Translated & with a Preface by
Iain Galbraith

**ARC**
PUBLICATIONS
2020

Published by Arc Publications,
Nanholme Mill, Shaw Wood Road
Todmorden OL14 6DA, UK
www.arcpublications.co.uk

Original poems copyright © Esther Dischereit, 2020
& Verlag Vorwerk 8, Berlin
Translation copyright © Iain Galbraith, 2020
Introduction copyright © Iain Galbraith, 2020
Copyright in the present edition © Arc Publications, 2020

978 1911469 70 4 (pbk)
978 1911469 71 1 (hbk)

ACKNOWLEDGEMENTS

The publishers are grateful to Verlag Vorwerk 8 for permission to reproduce poems from *Rauhreifiger Mund oder andere Nachrichten* and *Im Toaster steckt eine Scheibe Brot* by Esther Dischereit, both in the original German and in English translation.

The publishers and translator are grateful to the editors of the following journals and anthologies, in which some of the translated poems first appeared: *Dimensions2, Habitus, Ein Magazin über Orte, Sport, The Posen Library of Jewish Culture and Civilization Vol. 10 1973-2005, The Bitter Oleander, No Man's Land, World Literature Today.*

The translator is indebted to Irit Dekel and Michael Weinman for their insightful reading and guidance in several instances.

Design by Tony Ward
Printed •• •• ••• •• • •• •••• • •••• • •• •••• •• •,• • • • • • • • • • • • • • • •
•• •ᵱ •••• •• ••• •• •• •• • • • • • • • • • • • • • • • •

The translation of these poems was supported by a grant from the Goethe Institut which is funded by the German Ministry of Foreign Affairs.

'Arc Translations' series
Series Editor: Jean Boase-Beier

# CONTENTS

Translator's Preface / 7

*from*

ALS MIR MEIN GOLEM ÖFFNETE /
WHEN MY GOLEM OPENED UP (1996)

18 / 'Ich saß…' • 'I sat…' / 19
20 / 'Statt Milch haben wir…' • 'Instead of milk…' / 21
22 / Jüdische Renaissance I • Jewish Renaissance I / 23
24 / Jüdische Renaissance II • Jewish Renaissance II / 25
26 / 'Dünnwandig stand ich…' • 'Thin-walled I stood…'/ 27
28 / 'Chabibi…' • 'Chabibi…' / 29
30 / Deutsches Lied • German Lied / 31
32 / Mond und Blau • Moon and Blue / 33
34 / 'Ich kroch unter Berlin…' • 'I crept beneath Berlin…' / 35
36 / 'Weiche Wörter…' • 'Soft words…' / 37
38 / 'Meine Augen sind…' • 'My eyes have…' / 39
40 / Gefangen • Imprisoned / 41

*from*

RAUHREIFIGER MUND ODER ANDERE NACHRICHTEN /
HOAR-FROSTED MOUTH OR OTHER NEWS (2001)

44 / Grünstichige Rosen • Green-tinted Roses / 45
46 / 'Ich trage den Schnee…' • 'I carry my snow…' / 47
48 / 'Weiße Vögel rasen…' • 'White birds race…' / 49
50 / 'Manchmal segelt ein einzelnes • 'Sometimes a single leaf…' / 51
Blatt…'
52 / 'Der Tag riecht wie frische Minze…' • 'The day smells like fresh mint…' / 53
54 / 'Ich geh und lasse…' • ' I go, leaving…' / 55
56 / 'Ich springe durch…' • 'I leap through…' / 57
58 / 'Im Schlossturm von Darmstadt…' • 'In the Darmstadt Palace Tower…' / 59
60 / In den Steinen der Synagoge… • 'In the stones of the synagogue…' / 61
62 / 'Ein heißer Sommer…' • 'A hot summer…' / 63

*from*
## Im Toaster steckt eine Scheibe Brot / There's a Slice of Bread in the Toaster (2007)

66 / 'Im Toaster...' • 'There's a slice...' / 67

68 / Fähre nach Wannsee – • Ferry to Wannsee – then On / 69
dann weiter

70 / 'Sie kam aus der Ankunfts- • 'She came from the arrivals
halle...' hall...' / 71

72 / 'Der Mond...' • 'The moon...' / 73

74 / 'Heute waren sie gekommen...' • 'They had come here today...' / 75

76 / Ich find das komisch • I Find That Kind of Funny / 77

82 / Plötzensee Strand • Plötzensee Beach / 83

86 / Marina Bay's • Marina Bay's / 87

90 / Klappernde Silver Towers • Rattling Silver Towers / 91

96 / 'Erstaunt, fast erschrocken...' • 'Astonished, almost shocked...' / 97

100 / Ich renne über die Putlitzer • I Rush Across Putlitz Bridge / 101
Brücke

## Neue Gedichte / New Poems

110 / 1866 Gasthaus zum Lamm • The Lamb Inn, 1866 / 111

114 / 'Meinen Rücken...' • 'Stalks of grass...' / 109

116 / Kissing Terry in the Rain • Kissing Terry in the Rain / 111

118 / Über das Fahren im Schnee • On Travelling in the Snow / 113

120 / Gąski • Gąski / 115

122 / Nachwachsende Zeugen • Renewing Witnesses / 117

124 / 'Wir fuhren...' • 'We drove...' / 119

126 / 'Die Körper der Oliven...' • 'The bodies of the olives...' / 121

128 / 'Das Kleid der Zitronen...' • 'The frocks of the lemons...' / 123

130 / Die Gewesenen • The Once-weres / 125

Biographical Notes / 132

A little over halfway into Esther Dischereit's second volume of poems, *Rauhreifiger Mund oder andere Nachrichten* (Hoar-frosted Mouth or Other News, 2001), comes a one-line poem consisting of seven words: 'Ich geh und lasse meine Splitter liegen' (literally: I go and leave my splinters lying). The abrupt appearance of this poem's narrator is nothing if not wayward – someone, a first person singular, far from entering the scene is already leaving, making a break for it, signalling a fragmentary future. No less importantly, the poem announces a strategy of resistance – against extinction: the subject breaks but / and departs, while the part of her that had already come apart is left behind. Against abjection, the subject has the fortitude to survive the force that precipitates her "splinters" and walk away. After fracturing she speaks for herself.

Many of Esther Dischereit's poems, and many of her sentences, leave a troubled trace on the reading consciousness. I find myself (sometimes in irritation) returning to her poems and looking at them from a different angle, forgetting or needing to forget the impressions of a previous visit. It is as if one were studying the several faces of a Cubist artwork (one of Dischereit's essays is entitled 'The Cubist Gaze: Who Writes when I Write?'), whose substance or assertion, one supposes, inheres in the many-faceted simultaneity of different aspects. Angled edges and surfaces break into the poems, sometimes into the syntax of a single sentence or phrase:

> it's neat and tidy here
> paddle boats and rowing boats
> for hire on Sundays
> they hanged them in their underwear
> filmed the whole thing
> sitting at the bistro table two women
> drinking wheat beer
>
> (from 'Plötzensee Beach', p. 79)

The reading eye stumbles, forced to reorient in a suddenly precarious environment (rip currents, mixed messages). The banality of the tidied surface splits, an abyss opens: one of Berlin's shallow graves.

How then shall I translate the German sentence into English? Perhaps: "I go, leaving my splinters behind me". But is this even a poem? A generic subtitle on the cover of the book tells us the volume contains *Gedichte* (Poems), and we are nowhere told that this sentence makes an exception to the rule. And yet the book's title also speaks of *andere Nachrichten* (Other News): *Hoar-frosted Mouth or Other News* – not "and" but "or Other News". So in one sense the poems (which may themselves be the "splinters" she leaves behind) could also be read as news, or messages, or even intelligence (somewhat darkly, *Nachrichtendienst* usually means intelligence agency or secret service). They are "Other News" – so not the kind of news that buries what is really going on under "the latest" distractions put out by media corporations, but news that stands in some relation to the 'Hoar-frosted Mouth' of the book title: announcements made in a *hostile environment*, messages spoken to concern us now and tomorrow, news that will stay news.

In an interview, the Scottish poet Edwin Morgan spoke of the "writer or the poet being in receipt, if you like, of messages, just like people listening for stars' messages... Nothing is not giving messages, I think."[1] Here is Esther Dischereit, also in an interview and also speaking of the ubiquitous resources and insistence of messages: "To me, being Jewish meant engaging in the huge struggle of not speaking but listening. Listening to the tones of my voices, which would enable me to decode the unspoken voices. The voices of the dead, the

---

[1] "'Nothing Is Not Giving Messages". An Interview with Robert Crawford. 1988', in: Edwin Morgan: *Nothing Not Giving Messages*, edited by Hamish Whyte (Edinburgh: Polygon, 1990), p. 131. (N.B. The translations of passages cited in this introduction are my own.)

silent voices of the living… and the messages of things."[2] The objects that are found in our daily lives, she says in another interview[3], "become charged. What happens when things give each other the kiss of life – behind our backs – a village, a street, the rain, history entering them uninvited." Here is a sensibility to the aura of things: a subject knows what it is to be an object listening to the messages of other things which, given certain circumstances (an open ear), can respond or transmit. The Cubist gaze is one that animates the exchange between inside and outside, person and thing, subject and object. Esther Dischereit's poems not only listen to things intently, but enact the transformation of subjects (or at least first persons singular) into objects and vice versa. This awareness of the edges and aspects of things, the negations, ruptures and endings of voices, imbues the grammar of her poetry.

But who is this frangible "I" that leaves splinters behind her as she goes, and whose leaving them may be considered "news"? What can be said of her "splinters"? And what has prompted her leaving? It appears that the "I" of the poem is leaving (whether by necessity or choice or both) after some drastic event – a collision, or act of violence against the body. At the same time, we cannot in this case be "in receipt" of a message from any soft creature or thing because, at least in the most literal sense, these may tear or split but cannot, as a result of violent impact, shatter into splinters. Splinters tend to be hard and thin and often sharp, unlike mammalian body parts. But who says the speaker is a mammal? Perhaps the subject of the sentence, subject that is to violence, humiliation or intended annihilation, already consisted of splinters, and whatever has left the scene is something else

[2] '"Gelebte Zeit und aufgeschriebene Zeit" Ein Interview mit Astrid Deuber-Mankowsky' (Lived Time and Recorded Time), in: Esther Dischereit: *Mit Eichmann an der Börse* (Berlin: Ullstein, 2001), p. 153.

[3] 'Self-Interview by Esther Dischereit – Based on a Conversation with Sonja Fritzsche and Jennifer Good', in: *Women in German Yearbook* 2007. Vol. 23, p. 6.

– a voice? It's as if by the time we readers reach the scene she's as good as gone: we glimpse the splinters and feel the swirl, the displacement of air as she departs. The splinters, however, lie where they fell; following, we may cut our feet.

That said, if we introduce a context and zoom out just a little, we may find that the poem or sentence reflects a pivotal moment in Esther Dischereit's voluminous œuvre of novels, poetry, short stories, essays, works for radio, stage and screen, performances and installations. It is pivotal because, resembling a memory or recurring dream or compulsively repeated action, the recorded single sentence traces the trajectory from a position before to a position after the possibility of writing (or speaking): it crosses a threshold of speech that is predicated on the protracted effort of listening, decoding, bodying forth.

Thresholds are recurrent in Dischereit's work. The poem that opens the present volume, too, the opening poem in Dischereit's first volume of poetry, *Als mir mein Golem öffnete* (When my Golem Opened Up, 1996), presents an encounter with the "Golem" at a threshold. The Golem, in Jewish and Central European mythology, has always been an ambiguous figure, a protector and slayer of Jews. In this poem, seen from a "Cubist" perspective, so to speak, the Golem is no less complex than the role it adopts elsewhere in European literature: here we may see it as representing a Jewish "I"-persona's internalization of anti-Semitic attributions of malevolent superhuman powers; in a ploy to spite the objectifying and exclusive "you", the "I"-persona, who via the incorporation of the projected attributes has merged with the figure of the Golem, strikes out the letters on the Golem's forehead (that is, her own), reducing the Golem (that is, herself) to dust. Dust, like the "splinters", is all that is left behind. Anti-Semitism leaves no place for safety, balance or normality. As far as we can see, the "I" has not crossed the threshold, but there is a sense in which the world of the "you" has been left all the bleaker. There is also a promise of survival in the premise of narration: somebody has lived to tell the tale. On the one side: objectification and abjection; on the other: resilience in the face of expanding trauma.

Esther Dischereit was born and grew up in the small German town of Heppenheim, in South Hesse, to a Jewish mother who had survived the Nazi era in hiding before marrying a non-Jewish physician, with whom she had two daughters. In fact Esther, born in 1952, was her youngest daughter of three. A small number of Jews survived in hiding inside Nazi Germany, and here are five: Esther Dischereit's mother and first daughter, that is Esther's half-sister, her mother's first husband, and her mother's parents. They initially hid in Berlin where fear of discovery was continuous. This was not something that would end – even if by luck and cunning it did not end in annihilation – with German defeat and the family's liberation in 1945, as the ending of the poem 'I crept beneath Berlin' (p. 35) ominously suggests:

> One day we crept up the staircase
> into my frenzied heart
> for these last years
> and how much harder it beat
> careering after me to other countries
> until I came home to my cellar
> and was resolved.

Esther Dischereit's parents divorced when she was seven and her mother, until she died in a car accident when Esther was fourteen, brought up her two daughters alone amid memories, injustices and a political and cultural climate that showed the ingrained anti-Semitism of the Nazi era would not die easily.

A few sentences from Dischereit's acceptance speech on receiving the Erich Fried Prize in 2009 may offer a glimpse of the precariousness of this world without consolation or council:

> I later heard my sister speak of life before cancer and life after. This may seem inappropriate to you – we had our private way of reading time. Time before had come with us as a black vacuum. I didn't know what was inside

it. My mother, with whom we later lived on our own, was preoccupied with it, and struggled not to fall in. It showed itself again and again and hurled out – as if they were particles – fragments of unwelcome information... [4]

In an essay entitled 'On the Disappearance of Words', describing the time before she found a voice to write in, Esther Dischereit looks back at her childhood, and while capturing some of the speech she remembers (the double negatives) her evocation has recourse to words she could not have summoned then. Here, Dischereit decodes the messages of her "mother tongue", so to speak, a language not learned but received, incorporating its absences, silences and the knowledge of what must not be said. Perhaps it is not surprising then if, here again, we encounter her word "splinters":

> In my childhood there were splinters on the ground – of Auschwitz, Dachau, Bergen-Belsen. I saw them and touched them. Nobody noticed what I held in my hands. The other children didn't see no splinters and didn't touch none. Their parents knew of them but did not touch them. My parents knew of them and didn't want me to see them. So I began to ask myself whether this hand belonged to me. This was the beginning of self-abnegation, of doubting my own perceptions, my first experience of majority accord – deception. Is there a single body for the human being and the Jew, or shall I divide my face?[5]

Describing her childhood scene she finds a language that works as a kind of translation: an answer to the question raised by the French philosopher Antoine Berman (whose

---

[4] Esther Dischereit, Acceptance Speech on Receiving the Erich Fried Prize on 29 November 2009. Literaturhaus Wien: http://www. literaturhaus.at/index.php?id=6634
[5] 'Vom Verschwinden der Worte' (On the Disappearance of Words), in: Esther Dischereit, *Übungen, jüdisch zu sein* (Exercises in Being Jewish). (Frankfurt am Main: Suhrkamp, 1998), pp. 44-45.

Polish-Jewish-Yugoslav-French family also survived the Second World War in hiding): "comment rendre les paroles du matin avec les paroles du soir?"[6] (how do we account for the words of the morning with the words of the evening?).

Beyond the symbolic and metaphorical weight of this passage, and although she could barely have been aware of it at the time, it is true that during Esther Dischereit's childhood in Heppenheim there were "splinters" of concentration camps on the ground. Heppenheim, the home of Martin Buber from 1916 until the Nazis forced him into exile in 1938, had been the site of a Dachau sub-camp until December 1942, when the remaining Heppenheim Jews were deported to extermination camps. The camp was reopened in June 1943 as Heppenheim Sub-camp and remained active until 1945, when it was evacuated and the remaining prisoners were marched south to Dachau before the American army could cross the Rhein. A plaque marks the site of the former synagogue, destroyed in 1938; beside it a second plaque commemorates the names of 29 murdered Heppenheim Jews. An "insane asylum" in the southern outskirts of the town sent dozens of psychiatric patients to their deaths in the gas chambers in compliance with the so-called T4 (Euthanasia) programme. A German town not unlike others. It took Esther Dischereit many years to break through the barrier of projections, deceptions and self-doubt, first attempting to qualify as a teacher, a profession that was denied her by the powers that be, however, because, as a student, she had thrown in her lot with a communist organization – whose priorities, she felt, looking back, had left no space for the development of a writing self. Perhaps one clue to a breakthrough lay in the final sentence of the passage cited above: the question of a "single body for the human being and the Jew".

Esther Dischereit's first book of poetry *Als mir mein Golem*

---

[6] *La Traduction et la lettre ou L'Auberge du lointain* (1985). Éditions du Seuil (Paris: 1999), p. 83.

*öffnete* (When My Golem Opened Up, 1996) was not her first book. It was preceded by a children's book, *Anna macht Frühstück* (Anna Makes Breakfast, 1985) and the two novels *Joëmis Tisch* (Joëmi's Table, 1988) and *Merryn* (Merryn, 1992). The beginning of her first novel (if it is really a novel: it could just as easily be described as a book of "memory splinters"), contains the sentence: "After twenty years of being an un-Jew I want to become a Jew again." At the same time, her experience had taught her that it was impossible to return to pre-war Jewish traditions, a sentimentality dealt with ironically in her 'Jewish Renaissance' poems (pp. 23 & 25). Any notion of a Jewish identity would have to be one of her own making – mindful of the broken state of post-Shoah Jewish cultures and relations between Jews and Germans in particular, and licensed to criticize a politics of exclusion, displacement, ethnic cleansing, persecution and violence wherever it was perpetrated. Describing the explosive force of her breakthrough into writing in an interview, she has stated:

> *Joëmi's Table* is not a book of memoirs, but the overwhelming, violent incursion of history or memory into the present, similar to an eruptive event... I did not have to reach a certain age in order to write *Joëmi's Table*. There needed to be a waning of fear, fear of Nazi and post-Nazi society. And fear of a personal history one has only just struggled to drive back and keep at bay. I continued to be frightened even when the book appeared, expecting something terrible to happen at any moment. It was as if I had ended a life in illegality by exposing myself. I was, in a certain sense, ending the state in which my mother had lived, a survivor who had been banned during the Nazi era, a state she had passed on to me, born after 1945, as a part of my socialization.[7]

Besides the waning of her fear Dischereit mentions two other conditions that made it possible to begin writing.

[7] 'Gelebte Zeit und aufgeschriebene Zeit' Ein Interview mit Astrid Deuber-Mankowsky (Lived Time and Recorded Time), in: *op. cit.*, pp. 146-7.

One is the matter of the "single body": she could not have written if her relationship with her own body had not changed, ending her hostility towards it, repudiating her internalization of anti-Semitism and misogyny. Inability to inhabit the body imposes limitations on thought and the interaction of thought and feeling. The other factor was poetry. Sometimes, translating her poetry, one detects what one imagines to be echoes of Nelly Sachs, Paul Celan, Gertrud Kolmar, Erich Fried or Else Lasker-Schüler, only to be told that she did not read that author's work until after writing the poem in question. Sometimes one notices her reading: Shakespeare, or Sophocles, or the great Palestinian poet Mahmoud Darwish. As for thresholds, however, she has said that engaging with poetry was the most important route to finding her writing voice. Only when she had "found the courage to write poems, nothing but poems for a whole year", only when she had accepted poetry's "intimacy" and allowed her individuality full sway while seeing her own life "as one… among millions", was she able to write what she needed to write.

*Wiesbaden, August 2019*

15

*from*
ALS MIR MEIN GOLEM ÖFFNETE /
WHEN MY GOLEM OPENED UP
(1996)

Ich saß
vor deiner Tür
als
mir mein Golem
öffnete
führte mich
abseits
und strich
mir die Zeile
aus
jetzt fegst du
Staub
vor Deiner Tür

I sat
in front of your door
when
my golem
opened up
led me
aside
and struck
out
my letters
now you sweep
dust
in front of your door

Statt Milch haben wir
die Angst getrunken
sie wusch mir
die Augen weiß
dass ich niemals nicht
gesehen
wie ihr die Blumen seht

Ich seh die Blumen
wachsen in Dachau
es ist das schönste Foto
meiner Tochter

❦

Instead of milk
we have drunk fear
it washed
my eyes white
so I have not
never
seen the flowers as you do

I see the flowers
growing in Dachau
it's my daughter's
loveliest photo

## JÜDISCHE RENAISSANCE I

Wir wolln ein bisschen Aleph
und wolln die Mazze brechen
spielen Mütter, Urgroßväter
die haben wir nicht gesehen
sind nicht die Kinder von
wem und von woher

sie reden von uns wie
Ackerbauern von ihrer Erde

Straßenarbeiter hackten den
Bäumen in die Wurzel

Die Bäume schüttelten ihre Kronen
und blieben eine Weile lang stehen

Die anderen Bäume behaupteten
sie seien der Wald

Mir ist merkwürdig
wenn ich dazwischen gehe.

## JEWISH RENAISSANCE I

We want a bit of Aleph
and want to break the matzah
as if we were mothers, great grandfathers
we never saw
are not the children of those
from that place

They speak of us as
farmers do of their soil

Road workers hacked
into the roots of trees

The trees shook their crowns
and stood a while longer

The other trees claimed
they were the forest

To me it feels strange
walking in between.

## JÜDISCHE RENAISSANCE II

Übe das Tales tragen
sprich die Worte die nicht dir
sondern einer Ewigkeit gehören
such dir die Wahrheit auf der Stirn
schütze dich vor der Hand
die über die Buchstaben streicht
du brauchst jetzt Kraft
und sei sie nur geliehen

Eröffne ein Geschäft
mit dem Tafelsilber deines G'ttes
sieh zu dass du verkaufst
in der kurzen Blüte der Zeit
die bleibt
Ich bin schon tot
warum weigerst du dich
bei mir zu liegen
Niemand kann sich den G'tt
wie ein Bonbonglas kaufen

❧

## JEWISH RENAISSANCE II

Practice wearing the tallit
speak the words that belong not
to you but to eternity
seek for the truth on your forehead
beware the hand
that would rub out the letters
what you need now is strength
even if borrowed

Start a business
on the silverware of your G-d
make sure you sell
in the brief flowering of the days
you have left
I am already dead
why do you refuse
to lie beside me
Nobody can buy G-d
like a jar of candy

≈

Dünnwandig stand ich
zwischen denen, die
stehen stießen sich
an mir dann bückten
sie sich und
halfen mir
die Scherben aufzusammeln

Es ist dann kein Gefäß nicht
mehr aus mir geworden
blieb Ausstellungsstück
vergangener Zeit sodass
sie die Schulklassen
zu mir führten ganz dicht

Von deren Atem
fiel ich
vergiftet in den Staub

Ausgestrichen die Zeichen
auf der Stirn bin
ohne Anfang
ohne Ende

Jetzt haben sie Angst
vor mir als Staub

❧

Thin-walled I stood
among those who
stand who knocked
against me then
bent to
help me
gather the shards

I could never then
not ever become a vessel again
remained an exhibit
of a long gone time so
they brought their school classes
to view me close up

Because of their breath
I fell
poisoned to the dust

Struck out are the letters
on my forehead am
without beginning
without end

Now they're frightened
of me as dust

Chabibi
mein waibele
schütze dich
wenn du triffst
einen goj

der mag dich nicht

schütze dich
wenn du triffst
einen goj

der mag dich

schütze dich
wenn du triffst
einen jiden

der riecht dich

tanzen chassiden
in dein Herz
keine Mesuse
an deiner Tür
Mespochen
schneiden
dein Haar
dass es mit dem dibbuk
tanze

❧

Chabibi
my vaybl
be on your guard
when you meet
a goy

he likes you nisht

be on your guard
when you meet
a goy

he likes you

be on your guard
when you meet
a yid

he smells you

into your heart
dance chassids
no mezuzah
on your door
mishpoches
cut
your hair
so with the dybbuk
it will dance

## DEUTSCHES LIED

Ihr habt mich getaucht
in diese immerwährende Schwärze
ihr habt die Jüdin und das Mädchen
in euren Wänden aufgehängt
an meinen schwarzen Haaren
euer Glied gerieben

nach dem Mord besteigt ihr
eure Opfer

wie ihr sie liebt
die Toten

❧

## GERMAN LIED

You have drowned me
in this everlasting blackness
you have hung
the Jewess and girl within your walls
on my black hair
rubbed your members

after murdering you mount
your victims

how you love them
the dead

&

## MOND UND BLAU

Als der Mond heiß wird
verliere ich meine Schuhe
Die Augen laufen mir fort
leise rascheln die Laken
Auf blauem Grund mit grünen
Blumen
ertrinke ich.
Staub legte sich auf mein Haar.

## MOON AND BLUE

As the moon grows hot
I lose my shoes
My eyes desert me
soft swish of the sheets
On a blue ground with green
flowers
I drown.
Dust has settled on my hair.

Ich kroch unter Berlin
und lebte wie eine Ratte
vom Ausguss der Menschen
die um den Tisch herum saßen
beim Läuten der Glocken
zuckten wir zusammen
und hielten uns die jüdischen Ohren

Nach dem Verklingen der Kollekte
schwappten Milch und Brot von der Stiege
die eines Tages unter uns knarrte
Mein Gesicht hungerte vor Sonne
Der Luftzug zwischen den Dielen
verriet mir den heißen August
so schien es mir nach drei Mal Juni im März

Lagen zerknittert auf unseren Betten
in Anzug und Kleid und gelbgestrickter Weste
und waren den Büchern bereit für Gespräche
Ein Stampfen harter Schritte
lief uns über die Köpfe und Hand
versteckten wir uns
hinter dem Lid Seiner Augen

Eines Tages krochen wir die Stiege herauf
in mein rasendes Herz
auf die letzten Jahre
und schlug es immermehr laut
raste mir nach in die anderen Länder
bis ich heimkehrte in meinen Keller
und mich entschloss.

✸

I crept beneath Berlin
and lived like a rat
from the drains of the people
who sat round the table
When the bells tolled
we cowered and winced
and held our Jewish ears

When offertory noises faded
milk and bread sloshed from the staircase
which one day would creak under us
My face was starved for lack of sun
The draught through the floorboards
told me August was hot and here
so it seemed after three times June in March

Lying crumpled on our beds
in suits, dresses and a yellow knit waistcoat
we were ready to converse with the books
A pounding of hard steps
passed over our heads and hands
we hid
behind the lid of His eye

One day we crept up the staircase
into my frenzied heart
for these last years
and how much harder it beat
careering after me to other countries
until I came home to my cellar
and was resolved.

Weiche Wörter
verstopfen
mir den Mund
schlagen
mir mein Ohr
umschlingen
Arm und Beine
verknoten
Hände im Gelenk
bis
mir die Finger
spröde sind

Auf die Brücke
stellst
du Stühle
mir vor den Fuß
und auf die Hände
gibst
du mir zu tanzen
Stühle
treten
meine Augen
Mein Mund
verblutet
an den
weichen Wörtern

❧

Soft words
choke
my mouth
bash against
my ear
entangling
my arms and legs
keeping my wrists
tied
until
my fingers
are chapped

On the bridge
you place
chairs
in front of my feet
and on my hands
you give me
something to dance about
chairs
step
on my eyes
My mouth
bleeds out
on
soft words.

Meine Augen sind
vertrocknet
ich hab ein Meer
geweint
Du hast an den Haaren
mich gezogen
über viele Jahre weit
da sind sie schließlich
mitgewachsen
ich flocht sie dir
und deine Hand mit ein
sie sollten bald darauf
geschnitten sein

My eyes have
run dry
an ocean
I have wept
You dragged me
by the hair
for many long years
and ever longer
did it grow
I braided it for you
and braided your hand in too
soon after
it would be cut

## GEFANGEN

Sonne zerteilt unseren Morgen
Gegen Mittag bin ich gebrannt
Das frühe Geschwätz der Vögel
Wandelt sich in Lärm und Schreie
Schüchterne Knospen öffnen sich
Ausladend in den Hüften
Die Zartheit des Morgens
Hängt im Stacheldraht der Wiesen
Entsetzter Stein türmt sich
Mir ins Auge und kündet
Vom Hahnenschrei aus den Zellen.
Wie sinnlos trägst du deinen Kamm.

❧

## IMPRISONED

The sun dissects our morning
By midday I am burnt
The early chatter of birds
Turns to noise and screams
Shy buds burst
Wide in the hips
The tenderness of the morning
Hangs in barbed wire in the meadows
Horrified stones rear
Into my eyes bearing witness
To the cock's scream from the cells.
How pointless wearing your comb.

41

*from*
RAUHREIFIGER MUND
ODER ANDERE NACHRICHTEN /
HOAR-FROSTED MOUTH
OR OTHER NEWS
(2001)

## GRÜNSTICHIGE ROSEN

sah ich in einem eisweißen Garten
stehen das Winterlicht
hatte die gelbe Rose
mit ihrem Stengel gefärbt
sag nicht
es ist eine wundersame Sorte
damit ich nichts mehr
zu staunen hätte
sie wuchs in
einer Höhe als eine einzige
am Rand einer Straße
und doch wagte es
niemand sie an den Flügeln
zu stutzen
Sie kam mir entgegen
wie eine Geliebte
und hielt inne.

## GREEN-TINTED ROSES

I saw in an ice-white
garden the winter light
had coloured
the yellow rose and its stalk
don't say
it's a marvellous strain
leaving me nothing
to marvel at
it grew to
some height on its own
by the side of a road
yet nobody
dared
clip its wings
It came to me
like a lover
holding her breath.

Ich trage den Schnee
in einer Schale
zu Dir
Du stichst Höhlen
und Gassen hinein
setze dich nicht
und schlafe nicht ein
warnten die Stimmen
Du bist nach draußen
gegangen.

I carry my snow
to you
in a bowl
You riddle it
with caves and alleys
do not sit down
do not sleep
the voices warned
And you went
outside.

≋

Weiße Vögel rasen
auf mich zu
umschlingen
Arm und Beine
picken mir
Körner aus dem Gesicht
sind meine Tränen
die Landschaft gefriert
eine rote Girlande
schlängelt sich
über die Wiesen
ich ziehe sie hinter mir her
brauch dieses Pfand
und halte es dicht
vor die geränderten Augen
wir warten und
halten die Sehnsucht beisammen

White birds race
towards me
wrapping
my arms and legs
pecking the
seeds from my face
they are tears
the land freezes
a red garland
weaves its way
across the fields
me pulling it
needing this pledge
holding it close
to my ringed eyes
we are waiting
holding our longing together

Manchmal segelt ein einzelnes Blatt
zu Boden von Luftschlieren gefangen
und wieder freigegeben
ich tanze dem Blatt hinterher
und kann mir die Schritte nicht merken
ich strauchele, rudere mit den Armen
das Blatt wird nicht wieder fliegen
wie dies eine Mal
kein Blatt wird fliegen wie dies eine.
Hab ich dir neulich gesagt.

Sometimes a single leaf
sails to the ground, caught
by an air plume and released
I dance after the leaf
and cannot remember the steps
I falter, arms flailing
the leaf will not fly again
as it did this once
no leaf will fly like this one.
As I recently told you

Der Tag riecht wie frische Minze
am Morgen hast du die Lider bewegt
mir ins Gesicht gesehen
und auf die Hände
Ich trat auf die Straße
helle Sprenkel fielen auf mich
Leute berührten mich an
der Schulter
Ich sah irgendwohin
betrat einen Laden
Sonnenflecken auf den Stufen
die hinunter führten
Am Ausgang der U-Bahn
stieg ich hinauf
Eine Frau mit einem Bündel
frischer Minze
schob ein Fahrrad vorüber.
Eine Weile ging ich
hinter ihr her.
Auf ihrem Korb sah ich
deine Hände liegen.

The day smells like fresh mint
you raised your eyelids this morning
looked into my face
and at my hands
I went out on the street
dappled light fell on me
People touched
my shoulder
I looked elsewhere
entered a shop
There were sunspots on the stairs
leading down
I climbed the steps
to the subway exit
A woman with a bunch
of fresh mint
was pushing a bicycle along.
I walked behind her
for a while.
I saw your hands
resting in her basket.

Ich geh und lasse meine Splitter liegen

I go, leaving my splinters behind me

Ich springe durch
die Jahre und Jahrhunderte
und bin jetzt hier
ganz nah
fast gestern
Ein Stein lockt
die Fußspitze
wippt leicht
duftet die Luft
Hände die schmecken
ohne Zeit oder Raum
sozusagen eben

I leap through
the years and centuries
and now am here
so close
almost yesterday
A stone tempts
the tip of my toe
jigs a little
scent on the air
hands that taste
without time or space
just then, so to speak

Im Schlossturm von Darmstadt
hängt meine Zeit
ich lese Zeit
ich bin der Fürst von Hessen-Nassau
führe den Zeitkalender
dann läute ich zur Vesper
Seit sie die Zeit an jedermann
verkaufen
sehne ich mich
nach der gewölbten Zeit
in der ich sitzen könnte
Platz nehmen wie im Kino
mit Mozart oder Janis Joplin
Die Zeit benimmt sich wie
ein Vakuum
Ist sie Materie oder Nichts?
Die Zeit hat keinen Sinn
sie hat Materie
Grasbüschel in tickenden Einheiten
Meine Eltern sagten,
ich sollte die Grasbüschel nicht ausreißen.

❧

In the Darmstadt Palace Tower
hangs my time
I can read time
I am the Prince of Hessen-Nassau
I keep the calendar of the times
and so I ring for vespers
Since they began to sell time
to all and sundry
I have longed
for vaulted time
where I could sit
and take my place as at the movies
with Mozart or Janis Joplin
Time behaves like
a vacuum
Is it material or nothing?
Time has no meaning
it has material
tufts of grass ticking in units
My parents told me
not to tear out the tufts of grass.

❦

In den Steinen der Synagoge
stecken weiße Papiere,
die ich nicht abgeschickt
habe. Ein junger Mensch tritt ein.
Die Stimme der
Sängerin klingt
in den Räumen.
Orgelmusik
treibt Inn und Donau herauf.
Worauf warte ich eigentlich?

≲

In the stones of the synagogue
are bits of white
paper I have not
sent. A young person enters.
The woman's voice
singing
resounds through the rooms.
Organ music
drifts up Inn and Danube.
So what am I waiting for?

≈

Ein heißer Sommer
es war ihnen kalt
ein kalter Winter
sie sind verbrannt
ihre Schreie
trieben im Wasser
vor den Küsten
hinter denen ihr
Blumen und Gemüse anbaut
ihr würdet jetzt gern
das Gemüse uns schenken
und Blumen bringen
an den Tagen
an denen ich einzöge
um eine Nachbarin zu sein
Ich ziehe nicht ein
wer anders zieht ein
und ich bleibe die Nachbarin
die nicht einzog.

A hot summer
they were cold
a cold winter
they burnt
their screams
floating in the water
off the coasts
behind which you
plant flowers and vegetables
now you'd like to
give us the vegetables
and bring us flowers
on the days
when I would move in
to become your neighbour.
I won't be moving in
someone else is moving in
and I'll stay the neighbour
who didn't move in.

≋

*from*
IM TOASTER STECKT EINE SCHEIBE BROT /
THERE'S A SLICE OF BREAD IN THE TOASTER
(2007)

Im Toaster
steckt eine Scheibe Brot
es gibt Milch und Eier
Ich öffne und
schließe
den Kühlschrank
Regen fällt
hinter dem Fenster
und lässt Schlieren
zurück

❧

There's a slice
of bread in the toaster
there are milk and eggs
I open and
close
the fridge
Rain runs
down the window
leaving its streaks
behind

## FÄHRE NACH WANNSEE – DANN WEITER

Licht über dem Wasserspiegel
mit der Fahrkarte für die S-Bahn
die Leute packen Feuerwerkskörper
ins Boot und ein paar ihre Brote
die Passagiere fahren bis zur Hüfte
versunken im See
nur die Arme bleiben über Wasser
wer draußen sitzt,
kann eine rauchen
Käsekuchen auf Schweizer Art
sagte der Mann und goss
die türkischen Gläser auf
früher war er bei Osram
seine Familien saßen
auch im Cafe und schauten zu
wenn ein Fremder 'ne Bockwurst wollte
Manchmal stand einer auf und
half eine Tasse Kaffee zu machen.
Salsa kam aus der Steckdose
Weihnachtskugeln neben dem Kühlschrank
aufgeschichtet wie riesige
Rumtrüffel die Sekt- und Biergläser
trugen Geweihe. Toilette für
Nicht-Kunden -,50 Cent.
Ich zweifle, ob ich den Ort wiederfinde.
Vielleicht ist er das nächste Mal
nicht mehr da.

## FERRY TO WANNSEE – THEN ON


Light across the surface of the water
with the S-Bahn ticket
people are stowing fireworks
in the boat and some their sandwiches
the passengers travelling up to their hips
in the lake
only their arms still above water
if you sit outside
you can have a smoke
cheesecake Swiss-style
said the man and filled
our Turkish glasses
he used to be at Osram
his families were sitting
in the café too and watched
when some stranger wanted a bockwurst
Now and then one of them got up
to help with the coffees.
There was piped Salsa
Christmas baubles next to the fridge
stacked like giant
rum-truffles the champagne and beer glasses
had antlers. Restroom for
non-clients 50 cents.
I doubt I'll find this place again.
Perhaps next time
it won't be here.

Sie kam aus der Ankunftshalle
lächelte und hielt die Augen gesenkt
ich hatte vergessen
wie schön sie war
ich ging nahe zu ihr
und legte mein Gesicht an ihre Haare
ich atmete ihren Geruch
es gab nichts
das ich hätte wissen müssen

❧

She came from the arrivals hall
smiling, her eyes downcast
I had forgotten
how lovely she was
I went up to her
pressed my face to her hair
and inhaled her smell
there was nothing
I needed to know

☙

Der Mond
tauchte
durch deine geschlossenen Augen
ich weiß nicht wie du heißt
als die Nacht in deinen Armen lag
nahm ich die Küsse mit

The moon
dived
through your closed eyes
I do not know your name
while the night lay in your arms
I stole these kisses

❧

Heute waren sie gekommen
Die Männer nahmen Platz
auf zehn Stühlen
Ich drehte den Schlüssel
im Schloss.
Als die Tür aufsprang,
trugen sie schon die Thora.
Sie boten mir das glänzende Silber an.
Ich küsste es.
Dann flogen sie davon.
Lehmig und schwer
drang Erde durch die Ritzen
Mein Mund berührte die Wände
Sie waren aus Salz
Ihre Kissen lagen auch da

❧

They had come here today
The men had taken their places
on the ten seats
I turned the key
in the lock.
When the door sprang open
they were already holding the Torah.
They offered me the shining silver.
I kissed it.
Then they took flight.
Heavy as clay
earth pressed through the cracks
My mouth touched the walls
They were made of salt
Their cushions were there too.

## ICH FIND DAS KOMISCH


Ich find das komisch
Wenn ich meine Eltern frag
war'n die nicht dabei
die waren glatt zu jung

Ich find das komisch
wenn ich meine Oma frag
war die nicht dabei
die hatte viel zu tun
Sie wissen, harte Zeit

Ich find das komisch
wenn ich meinen Opa frag
war der nicht dabei
der war doch bloß im Krieg
und das ist
doch schon so lange vorbei

Ich find das komisch
wenn ich nach euren Nachbarn frag
da wart ihr nicht zuhause
und sowieso recht anders
und grad an diesem Tag
Ich find das komisch

Ich suche die Toten
meiner Heimatstadt
und find kein Grab für sie
die waren in Theresienstadt…
das stimmt dann wieder ohne Frage
da wart ihr nicht dabei

## I FIND THAT KIND OF FUNNY

I find that kind of funny
When I ask my parents
they say they weren't around
they were way too young

I find that kind of funny
When I ask my grandma
she says she wasn't around
she was much too busy
you know, tough times

I find that kind of funny
When I ask my grandpa
he says he wasn't around
he was just at war
and that's
such a long time ago

I find that kind of funny
When I ask of your neighbours
then you weren't at home
and anyway quite different
and on that very day
I find that kind of funny

I'm looking for the dead
of my home town
and can't find a single grave
they were in Theresienstadt…
no doubt about it
you weren't around

Opa sagt, nun hör schon auf
wir hatten's alle schwer
die Lebensmittel knapp
die Bomben und dann jede Nacht
da frag ich mich
wenn die jetzt alle Opfer war'n
wer hat es denn getan

Wir sind das Volk der Leider
und wie's dann ausgelitten war
da ging es drüben weiter
das Opfer wog so doppelt schwer
nimm das zur Kenntnis bitte sehr
Ich find das komisch

Und wie ich so durch unsre Wohnung geh
und wische Staub, hab dann einmal
das schöne Wandbild umgedreht
da stand es auf der Rückwand drauf
ein Rosengold – ein wenig blass
Ich sage, schau doch mal
ins Stammbuch rein
wer sollen Rosengolds denn sein?
Ich find das komisch

Mama sagt, sie weiß das nicht
und dieses schöne Stück
hat sie uns durch den Krieg
gerettet
doch unsre vielen anderen Sachen
die musste sie zuhause lassen

Grandpa says, enough of that
we all had it hard
food was scarce
and bombs every night too
now I ask myself
if all of them were victims
who were the ones who did it

We're the people who suffer
and when we were over our troubles
it went on 'over there' only rougher
in short our victimhood doubled
keep that in mind if you please
I find that kind of funny

And cleaning our flat one day
doing the dusting I turned
that lovely painting round
and there it was on the back
Rosengold – though somewhat pale
so I say, let us get out
the family tree, for who
can these Rosengolds be?
I find that kind of funny

She has no idea, my Mama says
and that lovely piece
she'd saved for us
kept it all through the war
but all the rest
she couldn't bring west

Hals über Kopf, Nacht über Tag
sie wüsste gar nicht
was ich frag
Ich find das komisch

Vom schönen Silber allzumal
ist nur der Kaffeelöffel hier geblieben
alles, alles blieb doch drüben
Ich sage, Mama, ach dieser Löffel
mit dem Monogramm HR
wer war denn das
ich wüsst' es gern
Sei still, mein Kind, es ist doch schon
so lange her
und außerdem – und außerdem
erinnere ich mich nicht mehr
Ich find das komisch

it was head over heels overnight
she couldn't see quite
what I wished to find out
I find that kind of funny

A coffee spoon is all that's left
of our beautiful silverware
the rest had to stay back there
I ask, what of this spoon Mama
the one with the initials HR
who was that
I'd like to know
Be quiet, my child, it really is
so long ago
and anyway – and anyway
I'm sure I no longer know
I find that kind of funny

## PLÖTZENSEE STRAND

kostet am Abend 5 Euro 50
für die Familie, sonst sieben
also springen sie gegenüber
von der steinernen Wand
da kostet es nichts
paar Wege weiter
wurden sie hingerichtet
die vom 20. Juli und andere
gepflegt ist es hier
Tretboote und Ruderboote
im Sonntagsverleih
sie wurden in Unterwäsche
gehenkt und dabei gefilmt
am Bistrotisch sitzen zwei Frauen
und trinken ein Hefeweizen
eine spricht von der pommerschen Großmutter
und wie sie immer noch
voller Misstrauen steckt,
verstört ist
vor allem, was fremd ist
das Bier ist kühl und gut gezapft
kleine Wellen schlagen
unter dem Balkon auf
wo die Frauen reden
Montag früh ist es hier
menschenleer und die Woche lang
bleibt es so
da bleiben nur die Hingerichteten
bis zum Wochenende
wenn die Kühlboxen gebracht werden
die Sonnenschirme und Strandkörbe.
Strandkörbe gleich hinter wedding drive

## PLÖTZENSEE BEACH


costs 5 Euros 50 in the evening
for the whole family otherwise seven
so they jump in
off the stone wall opposite
where it costs nothing
few roads further down
is where they got executed
the *20 July* people and others
it's neat and tidy here
paddle boats and rowing boats
for hire on Sundays
they hanged them in their underwear
filmed the whole thing
sitting at the bistro table two women
drinking wheat beer, one
talking about her grandmother from Pomerania
of how she is still
deeply suspicious
distraught more like
especially anything foreign
the beer is cool and well drawn
tiny waves lap on the shore
under the terrace
where the women are talking
it's completely deserted here
on Monday mornings
and so it stays all week
the executed left to themselves
till the weekend
when the coolers come out
the beach umbrellas and beach chairs.
Beach chairs just after wedding drive

und Großmarkt Westhafen
wedding
natürlich wedding
wedding heißt doch Hochzeit oder nicht?

❧

and Westhafen Market
wedding
o yes wedding of course
wedding does mean wedding no?

❧

## MARINA BAY'S

Die Männer nahmen sie mit
nach Hause
unterwegs hielten sie an
und pinkelten
Schritte zurück folgten
die Söhne
und trugen ihnen die Bierdosen
und Angelruten nach
Niemals so viele gesehen wie heute
redeten sie
an den Steinmauern entlang
lagen die Tüten mit den zuckenden
Fischleibern darinnen
einer sprang
stieg nass wieder herauf
die Schwester hielt ihm
ihr Handy entgegen
ein Mann schlug Kopf
und Kiemen ab
die Kleine sah zu
und mochte es nicht.


Die Möwen schrien und
rannten auf den Mauern
verließen das Land
mit einem Flügelschlag
Ich sah die Jungen
sich kopfüber stürzen
unsere Augen nahmen sie
mit in die Tiefe der Wellen
drangen hastig in sie ein

## MARINA BAY'S

The men took them home
with them
stopping on the way
to pee
just steps behind
came their sons
carrying for them
their beer cans and fishing rods
Never seen as many as today
they said
along the stone walls
lay their plastic bags
with the twitching bodies of fish
one leaped in
came back up wet
his sister handed him
her cell phone
a man was cutting off
heads and gills
the little girl watched
and didn't like it.


The gulls screamed and
ran along the walls
leaving the land
with a beat of their wings
I saw the boys
dive in headfirst
they took our eyes with them
into the depths
entering them hurriedly

als sie heraufstiegen
klebten ihre Hosen
zwischen den Arschbacken fest
In den Nächten
war es auch so.


Unter dem Dach
der stadtwärtsstrebenden Möwen
duckten sie sich an
den Hauswänden entlang
der Regen hielt
die Leute zusammen
wie eine Schafherde
sie kuschelten mit den
Lieblingstieren ihrer Kinder
Molly trug ein Hemd
mit Spaghetti-Trägern
und einen Rock darunter
dann weiter nichts.
Und. Weiter nichts.


❧

when they climbed out
their trunks stuck
in the cracks of their buttocks
At night it was
like that too.


Under the ceiling
of townward-labouring gulls
they ducked along
the walls of houses
the rain keeping
people together
like a flock of sheep
they were cuddling their children's
favourite animals
Molly was wearing a shirt
with spaghetti straps
and a skirt under which
and that was it.
And. That was it.

## KLAPPERNDE SILVER TOWERS


geben uns abfließende
Duschwasser und Sirenen
in peitschenden Frequenzen
wir glauben an die Aufmerksamkeit
des doorman
der ID Karte
oder andere Behauptungen
dass es mich gibt

Stand in line –
die Kellnerin platziert
wir nehmen keine Pakete an
in weiß gepackten Papieren
seit zweihundert Jahren
„warum" sagte das Mädchen
„security" sagte die Angestellte
am Postamt Ecke Mercerstreet
und schloss
die Schalterhalle ab


Baumwollbüschel
lagern
in meinem Schlaf
färben mir die Stirn
wölben sich auf
über der Brust
verstopfen
dir Mund und Augen
ich treibe sie weg
mit den Stößen meines Atems

## RATTLING SILVER TOWERS

give us draining
shower waters and sirens
at punishing frequencies
we believe in the attentiveness
of the doorman
the ID card
or other such claims
that I exist

*Stand in line –*
the waitress places us
we have not accepted packages
wrapped in white paper
for two hundred years
*why* asked the girl
*security* said the worker
at the Mercer Street post office
and locked up
the teller hall


Tufts of cotton
collect
in my sleep
colouring my forehead
swelling
over my chest
plugging
your mouth and eyes
I drive them away
with my panting breath

sie kommen wieder
zurück
bis sie in Säcken
gepackt sind
und verschnürt.


Ächzende Häuser
biegen sich unter
dem Mann der
kopulierend übereinander
Beethoven am Sonntag
beim Zusammenlegen
ihrer Unterhosen
im Wäschekeller
sieht der doorman
in die Kamera
und wird unter
der Uniform steif

Sie dreht sich
zum Auge
und wechselt
ihre Wäsche
unter den Jeans
in der Ecke
strömt feuchte Luft
aus einem rostigen Hahn

they keep
coming back
until they are stuffed
into sacks
and tied up.


Groaning houses
bend under
the man who
copulating on top of each other
Beethoven on a Sunday
in the basement laundry
she's making a pile
of her panties
and the doorman
watching through the camera
grows hard
under his uniform

She turns
to face its eye
and changes
her underwear
under her jeans
in the corner
damp air streams
from a rusty valve

Wenn sie die Wäsche
herausnimmt
und während sie tropft
dreht sich
ihr Hintern heraus
und der ein Stockwerk über ihr
lässt seine Augen
über den Keller gleiten
es gibt einen Mauervorsprung
darunter ein Abflussgitter
über dem sie hockt
er weiß es

wegen ihres Schuhs
der hervorragt aus der
Mauerecke
seine Uniformhose
trägt scharf gebügelte Falten
er steht auf
der rostige Hahn strömt
feuchte Luft aus
in regelmäßigen
Stößen

❧

While she removes
her laundry
and lets it drip
her butt
sticks out
and the guy one floor above
lets his eyes
glide through the basement
there's a projecting wall
below it a drain grate
over which she's hunkered down
he knows it

because of her shoe
protruding from the
edge of the wall
his uniform pants
are sharply creased
he stands up
the rusty valve blows
damp air
in regular
bursts

I

Erstaunt, fast erschrocken
über den Schnee in der Wüste
dem sie barfuß begegnen
türmt sich die Weiße auf
den flachen Dächern der alten Städte
mit ihren Wagen fahren sie
das seltene Nass in die Täler hinab
gaben es den Frauen
zum Geschenk für den Abend


II

Ich brachte den Schnee
von Maaloula nach Jerusalem
darauf zogen sie Jesus Kleider an
Mäntel aus Armeebeständen
die Kugeln wurden gefüllt
Kinder aßen davon als Eis
und verdarben in den Lagern
wann werden die Steine schmelzen
in Jerusalem?


III

An diesem Tag
rieb ich ihr Gesicht
bis es heiß und gerötet war
Sie lachte
mit ihrem hellen Gelächter
das ich so liebe
Die Flocken schmolzen

I

Astonished, almost shocked
by the snow in the desert
which they encounter barefoot
the white heaping up
on the flat roofs of the old towns
they descend into the valleys
with this rare wetness in their cars
presenting it to their womenfolk
as an evening gift


II

I took the snow
from Maaloula to Jerusalem
then they dressed Jesus
army stock coats
they filled the balls
children ate them as ice-cream
and perished in the camps
when will the stones melt
in Jerusalem?


III

That day
I rubbed her face
until it was hot and flushed
She laughed
with the bright laughter
I love so much
The flakes melted

auf ihrem Hals
und liefen den Nacken hinunter


IV

Nicht Bomben
die aus dem Himmel fallen
Dieselgeruch hängt über den Straßen
vom Heizen in den Häusern
die an die Sonne gewöhnt
Ich habe Hoffnung,
dass es ein langer Winter bliebe

Bis mir die Steine schmelzen
Bis mir die Steine schmelzen

in Jerusalem

on her neck
and ran down her nape


IV

Not bombs
falling from the sky
a smell of diesel hangs over the streets
from the heating in the houses
so used to the sun
It is my hope
this winter will last

till I see the stones melt
till I see the stones melt

in Jerusalem

## ICH RENNE ÜBER DIE PUTLITZER BRÜCKE

Die Vorübergehenden
schlagen sich ab
mit ihren Gerüchen
an meinem Gesicht
Rasierwasser und Parfüms

Wenn ich abwärts schaue
ich schaue abwärts
auf das Stein- und Geröllbett
der Gleise in weiten Schlingen
aus der Ferne nähern sich
Züge und Waggons
wie aus dem Spielzeugkasten
ich bin wieder gerannt
auf der Mitte schneller
von hier fallen Frauen und
Männer in Kostümen und Anzügen
durch die Streben des Geländers.
Die kleinen Mädchen sehen aus
als hielte sie Mary Poppins
an den Händen
sie fliegen mit ihr
Jeden Tag fallen die Leute
durch die Streben und fliegen abwärts
im Winter haben sie Mäntel an
Ich sage den Passanten nichts
sie laufen mit eiligen Schritten
dahin wo ein Tag beginnt
Die Leute schreien nicht
sie fallen von der Putlitzer Brücke
ich sehe sie am Morgen
es ist Morgen

## I RUSH ACROSS PUTLITZ BRIDGE

People passing
slough off
their smells
in my face
aftershave and perfumes

when I look down
I look down on the long
loops of the tracks
in their bed of stone and gravel
trains and wagons
approaching from afar
like out of a toy-box
I've been rushing again
quicker in the middle
where women and men
costumed or suited fall
through the bars of the parapet.
The little girls look
as if Mary Poppins
had taken them by the hand
they are flying with her
There are people who fall every day
between the bars and down they fly
in winter they wear coats
I say nothing to the passers-by
who are hurrying on
to where a new day begins
The people don't scream
they fall from Putlitz Bridge
I see them in the morning
it is morning

ich kehre zurück
an einem Feiertag
flackert eine Kerze am Boden
vor den Füßen einer Frau
sie hat feste Schuhe an
eine lavendelfarbene klotzige Kerze
in die Wachswand sind Muscheln
eingelassen, von der Nordsee
oder von der Ostsee
wenn der Wind schräg steht
wird es Wachstropfen geben
auf den festen dunklen Schuhen der Frau
soll ich auch eine Kerze bringen
die Frau wird in einem Rahmen
stehen zwischen den flackernden Dochten
sich nicht bewegen
nicht springen wie die anderen
Ich wache über meiner Kerze
damit sie nicht ausgeht
drehe mich um und sehe
zwei Männern nach
stehen lassen möchte ich rufen
stehen lassen
um Himmels willen
lassen Sie die Kerze stehen
sie stand bei einem Mädchen
im Zimmer in der Nähe des Spiegels
die lavendelfarbene Kerze

sie muss nach mir gekommen sein
als ich weiterrannte
den Kanal entlang

I come back
on a public holiday
a candle flickers on the ground
at a woman's feet
she is wearing sturdy shoes
it's a chunky lavender-coloured candle
embedded in the wax
are shells from the North Sea
or from the Baltic
when cross winds blow
there'll be drops of wax
on the woman's dark and sturdy shoes
should I bring a candle too
the woman will stand there framed
between the flickering wicks
won't move
won't jump like the others
I keep an eye on my candle
so it doesn't go out
turn around
watching two men pass
leave that alone I want to shout
leave it alone
for Heaven's sake
leave that candle alone
it used to be in a girl's room
close to her mirror
that lavender-coloured candle

she must have arrived here after me
when I ran on
along the canal

bückte sie sich und zündete ein Streichholz an
am nächsten Tag
legte ich Kiesel dazu
sie reiben aneinander
wenn die Frau ihre taub gewordenen Füße
bewegt
Es fällt mir schwerer zu laufen
sogar das Gehen macht Mühe
eines Tages werde ich ganz auf dieser
Uferseite bleiben.

Die Kerze war fortgenommen
noch nicht einmal ein Rest
war stehengeblieben
An den Seitenrändern
der Stele sieht es nach Kotze aus
Ich gucke hin
Am Morgen lag die Rose da
eine rote langstielige
später heruntergeweht
auf den Asphalt
anderntags wieder hochgelegt
sorgsam
ich lege mich zu der welk Gewordenen
der Wind treibt mich
herunter den eiligen Passanten
vor die Füße die rennen zu
einfahrenden Schnellzügen
hier oben hält niemand an
hier ist es kalt und windig
und hässlich vom Chemiegestank
der Fabrik und dem Müll

she bent and lit a match
on the following day
I added some pebbles
they rub together
when the woman shifts
her numbed feet
I find it harder to run now
even walking gives me trouble
one of these days I'll just stay
this side of the river.

Someone had taken the candle
not a bit of it
was left
Down the sides
of the stele something like vomit
I look down
The rose had been there that morning
red and long-stemmed
later blown
onto the pavement
on the following day put back
carefully
I lie down with this faded one
the wind blows me
down before the feet
of the passers-by
hurrying to incoming trains
up here nobody stops
it's cold and windy here
and noxious with the stench of chemicals
from the factory and garbage

auf dem Kanal
eine zugige Brücke kein Kiosk
zum Anhalten oder was
ich kann doch nicht
hier stehen bleiben
bis ich sie sehe
ich bin mir sicher
dass es eine Frau ist
ich weiß, dass sie es ist
sie muss es sein
sie arbeitet in der Nähe
ich bin mir sicher
dass sie es ist
falls sie hier aussteigt
ich könnte auch eine Blume
dorthin legen, das könnte ich
oder einen kleinen Stein
oder ein weißes Papier
das der Wind ins Maul nimmt

in the canal
a draughty bridge no kiosk
to stop for or anything
I can't just
stand here
until I see her
I am sure
it's a woman
I know it's her
it must be her
she works near here
I am sure
that it's her
if she gets out here
I too could lay down
a flower there, yes I could
or a small stone
or a scrap of white paper
for the wind to take in its mouth

❧

# NEUE GEDICHTE /
## NEW POEMS

Hinter den Judenhäusern
bis 1925 wohl noch
dann Amerika
ein Stein auf den Gräbern
des Judenfriedhofs
in deutschen Worten
und denen für Adonai, dem Herrn
in dem 60-Leute-Dorf
zwischen den Äckern und Hügeln
eine Stunde entfernt von der Stadt
leben zwei Sinti-Familien
ein Paar von der Grenze
die Frau von hier
er: von dort
und der Diamantenschleifer
aus Amsterdam geflohen
vor Isabella, saßen
später für den zwölfjährigen Jesus
im Tempel Modell oder standen
über Auschwitz nach Wameling
da wo die Straße
Hinter den Judenhäusern
heißt in Wameling mit Katze
und Hund neben dem grobkörnig
verputzten Haus der Nachbarin
bei der die betenden Männer
über der Schlafzimmerdecke
zu hören sind mit ihren alten Schuhen
es knarrt ein bisschen
wenn sie sich neigen
an den Samstagen
hört sie nicht will den Fremden

## THE LAMB INN, 1866

Behind the Jews' Houses
probably till around 1925
then America
a single stone on the graves
in the Jewish cemetery
with German words
and those for Adonai, the Lord
in this village of 60 inhabitants
between hills and fields
an hour from town
live two Sinti families
a couple from the border
the woman from here
he: from there
and the diamond cutter
from Amsterdam who took flight
from Isabella, they sat
later for the twelve-year-old Jesus
in the temple or stood
via Auschwitz to Wameling
just where the street
is called Behind the Jews'
Houses in Wameling with a cat
and dog by the rough-cast
walls of the neighbour's house
where men may be heard praying
above the bedroom ceiling
in their old shoes
it creaks a little
when they sway
on Saturdays she does not
hear them does not want to show

den Weg nicht zeigen
nie nicht kein Betsaal hier gegeben
will nicht nichts finden
unter dem Dachboden
die Lehrer daneben halten
die Jalousien geschlossen
im Dorf nebenan
wartet ein altgewordenes
Goebbels-Kind
Rosa vom Haus hinter den Judenhäusern
ist die aus Auschwitz
sitzt neben ihm
bei der Kirmes und hebt
ein schäumiges Bier
Die andere auch.
Sie schlürfen und wischen
die weißen Münder ab.
Auf dem Dachboden liegen
abgerissene Schulterstücke.

❧

these strangers the way no never
no prayer room here
does not want to find
nothing under that attic roof
the teachers next door
keep their blinds closed
in the neighbouring village
waits an aged
Goebbels-child
sitting next to her
at the parish fair
Rosa from the house behind the Jews' houses
is the one from Auschwitz
and raises a foaming glass of beer
as does the other.
They slurp and give
their white lips a wipe.
On the floor of the attic
lie torn-off epaulettes

Meinen Rücken
streichen Grashalme
und biegen sich fort
flüchtige Streifen
so als hätte ich geträumt
vorsichtig die Fingerkuppen
meiner Tochter
bevor sie ihrem Zimmer
entwächst

Stalks of grass
stroke my back
and bend away
a fleeting touch
as if I were dreaming
of my daughter's
fingertips wary
before she grows
out of her room

❧

Ich trat aus der Haustür
den Kaffee in der Hand
in der anderen einen Koffer
der Regen fiel in Schnüren
wie Perlen
sie platterten auf
den noch heißen Kaffee
ich hätte trinken können
den Kaffee mit den Tropfen darinnen
ich hielt den Becher fest
als wollte ich ihn füllen
mit Perlen
stellte den Becher
auf die Straße wohin sonst
auf das Trottoir
vor das wartende Auto

Wie er da stand und
der Regen in Schlieren
auf seinem Gesicht herunterlief
und sich zwischen uns zwängte
als wir uns küssten
sein Mantel schon vollgesogen
mein Hals und die Hände
von den Augen
fielen Regentropfen
wie Perlen er trug sie
ins Haus

## KISSING TERRY IN THE RAIN

I stepped out of the front door
a coffee in one hand
my case in the other
strings of rain fell
like pearls
pattering on
my still hot coffee
I could have drunk
the coffee with those drops in it
I clutched the mug
as if wishing to fill it
with pearls
put the mug down
on the street where else
on the sidewalk
in front of the waiting car

The way he stood there
rain streaking
down his face
pushing between us
as we kissed
his coat soaked
my neck and hands too
raindrops falling
like pearls from
my eyes he wore them
into the house

❧

## ÜBER DAS FAHREN IM SCHNEE

wenn die Arme dünn gestreckter Zweige
wie vergebliche Fingerzeige
in die Atemluft ragen
Vögel in Schwarz auffliegen
und sich niedersetzen
weiße Winde vor Fenstern flirren
Ein einzelner Baum auf der Höhe
sich widersetzt
kein Schneeweiß
kein Rosenrot
steht er da
und steht da
und immer nur da

Was stehst du Baum
und siehst
in die Felder
die Bäche und Flüsse
Mensch und Tier
die Luft steht steif gefroren
über deinen Ästen und
weist mir Wege
von welchen
die da gewesen waren

❦

## ON TRAVELLING IN THE SNOW

when the thin arms of stretching twigs
like futile pointing fingers
reach into the air we breathe
birds in black take wing
and settle again
white winds flutter at the windows
A single tree on the ridge
resists
no Snow-white
no Rose-red
it stands there
and stands there
always in the same place

Why, tree, do you stand
there gazing
into the fields
at rivers and streams
human and beast
the air frozen stiff
over your branches
showing me paths
once taken
by those who passed

## GĄSKI

Nachtschwarze Regen
stehen vor unseren klapprigen Fenstern
schließen uns ein wie lahme Vögel
deren Tage schwer tropfen
wenn Brot und Käse knapp werden
verlassen wir unsere Höhlen
und ducken uns an den Wolkengebirgen
vorbei in den Supermarkt
in dem wir bleiben
länger als nötig und uns beraten
über die Sorten und dies und den Keks
so als brächte uns der Ort einander näher
hält fest und zusammen mit anderen
die bleiben länger als nötig und beraten
über die Sorten und dies und den Keks
das Auto bringt uns fort
zurück zu den Häusern vor denen
die Nacht schwarz im Regen steht
und wir drinnen uns geschäftig hin und her
die Nacht und der Regen
füllen die Ritzen
quellen hinein und legen
Schlaf auf die Rücken.
Die Türen ließen wir angelehnt.

❧

## GĄSKI

The night-black rains
stand outside our ramshackle windows
shutting us in like lame birds
whose days drip heavily
when bread and cheese run out
we quit our caves
and ducking past mountains of cloud
make it to the supermarket
in which we stay
for longer than necessary seeking advice
on brands and that and the biscuit
as if the place had brought us closer together
holding us there with others too
who stay for longer than necessary and talk
of brands and that and the biscuit
the car takes us away
back to the houses in front of which
night stands black in rain
and while we bustle about inside
the night and the rain
fill the cracks
welling inside and covering
our backs with sleep.
We left the doors ajar.

≋

## NACHWACHSENDE ZEUGEN

Graue Schlieren
liegen über dem Gras
und auf den ausgebreiteten Röcken
über den Buchseiten
bedecken den Schuh
wenn du hineinschlüpfst
wie feiner Puder
auf Gesicht und Händen
du wäschst sie wieder und wieder
bedeckt dich der Staub
der Platz nimmt in deinem Haus
wie ein alter Bekannter
und bleibt.

## RENEWING WITNESSES

Grey streaks
lie across the grass
and on our outspread skirts
on the pages of books
covering your shoe
when you slip it on
like a fine powder
on your face and hands
which you wash again and again
the dust covers you
it settles in your house
like an old familiar
and stays.

❧

Wir fuhren
über uns Schwärme kleiner Vögel
wie dunkle Punkte und
markierten unseren Weg
durch die Luft
Du hieltest einen Kuchen
in deiner Hand
ich aß
drehtest die Töne auf
ich hörte
zeigtest auf die vom Regen
durchnässten Scheunen und Felder
ich sah
die lichten Nebel
deiner Länder
ich webe dich ein
und er webte mich ein
am Schalter war es spät
warum er die Sonnengläser
nicht abnahm
ich sah ein paar Krümel
wo ich gesessen hatte
und wie sich das Leder wölbte

We drove
above us flocks of small birds
like dark spots
marking our way
through the air
You were holding a cake
in one hand
I was eating
you turned up the volume
I listened
you pointed to the rain-drenched
barns and fields
I saw
the wispy mists
of your country
I am weaving you in
and he wove me in
we were late at the counter
why did he not
remove his sunglasses
I saw a few crumbs
where I had been sitting
and the way the leather bulged

Die Körper der Oliven
die Oliven der Körper
an einem der Fenster fehlt eine Olive
die Olive kann man nicht kaufen
sie ist handgemacht und alt
manchmal stehen Oliven im Krieg
sie werden dann Gefallene
ich liebe platzende Oliven
sie schützen meine Ohren
vor dem Donner der Gefechte
Es gibt keine weißen oder roten Oliven
der Olivenfabrik war die Farbe ausgegangen
dann nahmen sie die kriegsgrüne Farbe
bestrichen die weißen und roten damit
die wanderten mit den anderen in die Presse
es war ein Gift, das ich in der Pfanne erhitzte
viele Menschen starben
wir pflanzten weiter Plantagen
bestrichen mit kriegsgrüner Farbe
aus meiner Familie haben die Bäume überlebt
die Menschen liegen darunter.

❧

The bodies of the olives
the olives of the bodies
an olive is missing on one of the windows
you cannot buy the olive
it is handmade and old
olives are sometimes at war
they are the fallen then
I love bursting olives
they protect my ears
against the thunder of battle
There are no white or red olives
the olive factory ran out of paint
so they took war-green and painted
the red and white olives
these went in the press with the others
it was poison I heated in the pan
many people died
we continued to plant the orchards
using war-green paint
the trees in my family have survived
while my people lie underneath.

Das Kleid der Zitronen
gelbgenarbt
mit verblassenden Stichen
aneinander
aufeinander
vor- und übereinander liegend
wie die Familie
vor dem Auge der Kamera
seit Jahren
das feuchte Fleisch, umhüllt
von festen Schalen
im Dunkel der Kammer,
der Jahrhunderte
ein Haufen auf silberner Schale

Ich sah sie an in dieser Woche
und schmeckte ihren Saft.
Anonymos, 1655, Museo Nacional de Bellas Artes

❧

The frocks of the lemons
yellow-pored
with fading cuts
touching
lying on top of one another
before behind above
like the family
in front of the camera's eye
for years
the moist flesh – encased
in firm rinds
in the darkness of the larder
of the centuries
a heap in a silver bowl

I took a look at them this week
and tasted their juice.
Anonymos, 1655, Museo Nacional de Bellas Artes

❦

## DIE GEWESENEN

nicht einen Schritt kann ich tun
ohne den Gewesenen zu begegnen
die Frauen die eine Schirmmütze tragen
und Jogginghose die eine in pink
wissen das nicht, die Gewesenen
hinter und vor ihnen und begleiten sie
den Berg hinauf den sie mit ihren Kindern
besteigen, deren Fahrräder schiebend, wenn
sie noch klein sind
ach wirklich sagen sie
das ist interessant und kaum zu glauben
am Fuße des überwucherten Friedhofs
entkorken die Jungens ihre Biere, rauchen,
Musik, Hosen in Tarnfarben und kurz geschnittene
Haare, sehr kurz.
Die Gewesenen gehen mitten durch sie hindurch
es stört sie nicht einer rülpst sie sehen dem Wege
nach als sei da einer gegangen
es war aber nur ich

❧

## THE ONCE-WERES

I can't take a step
without falling in with the once-weres
the women wearing baseball caps
and joggers one in pink
do not know the once-weres
behind them, in front, walking beside
them up the hill with their kids
pushing the bikes of the ones
who are still small
oh really they say
well I never and unbelievable
at the foot of the overgrown graveyard
boys opening their beer-bottles, smoking
music, camo pants and close-cropped
hair, very close.
The once-weres walk straight through them
they're not bothered one burps they glance
at the path as if someone has passed
but it was only me

≋

ESTHER DISCHEREIT, described by her publisher, Suhrkamp
Verlag, as "possibly the preeminent German-Jewish voice
of the post-Shoah generation", was born in Heppenheim,
Germany, in 1952 and now lives in Berlin. She has published
fiction, poetry, and essays, and is a prolific writer for radio
and the stage. Her first novel *Joëmis Tisch – Eine jüdische
Geschichte* (Joëmi's Table – A Jewish Story), was published
by Suhrkamp in 1988. It was followed by the novel *Merryn*
(Merryn; Suhrkamp, 1992), two volumes of essays – *Übungen
jüdisch zu sein* (Exercises in Being Jewish; Suhrkamp, 1998)
and *Mit Eichmann an der Börse* (With Eichmann at the Stock
Exchange; Ullstein, 2001) – as well as by several volumes of
poetry: *Als mir mein Golem öffnete* (When My Golem Opened
Up; Stutz, 1996), *Rauhreifiger Mund oder andere Nachrichten*,
(Hoar-frosted Mouth or Other News; Vorwerk 8, 2001), *Im
Toaster steckt eine Scheibe Brot* (There's a Slice of Bread in the
Toaster; Vorwerk `8, 2007).

Dischereit's more recent publications include a collection
of short stories, *Der Morgen an dem der Zeitungsträger* (The
Morning the Paperboy; Suhrkamp, 2007) and *Vor den Hohen
Feiertagen gab es ein Flüstern und Rascheln im Haus* (Before the
High Holy Days the House was Full of Whisperings and
Rustlings; AvivA, 2009), the book adaptation of a sound-
installation conceived as a Holocaust memorial and tribute
to the former Jewish citizens of the city of Dülmen. Her
opera-project *Blumen für Otello. Über die Verbrechen von Jena*
(Flowers for Otello. On the Crimes of Jena), dedicated to
the victims and their families of a series of racist killings
perpetrated in Germany between 2000 and 2007, was
published by Secession Verlag in 2014 and premiered as
a radio play in 2014, when it was nominated for the ARD
Prize for Radio Drama. In August 2014 Dischereit's sound
installation *Particles of the Child with the Big Face* opened in the
MuseumsQuartier in Vienna. The installation in fact

drew on a longer prose narrative, published under the title *Grossgesichtiges Kind* (The Child with the Big Face; De Gruyter, 2015).

The founder of the avant-garde project WordMusic, Dischereit has also worked as a curator for various projects in contemporary art / new media. Her film *A Dress from Warsaw* – a co-production with director Mihał Otłowski – was shown at the Ashkelon Film-Festival "Jewish Eye" in 2008 and nominated for the Prix Genève in 2007.

She has been a Fellow at the Moses Mendelssohn Centre for European and Jewish Studies and the DAAD Chair for Contemporary Poetics at New York University (2019), and holds frequent lectures and readings in the United States, Canada, the Middle East, the Americas and Europe. In 2009 she received Austria's prestigious Erich Fried Prize for her writing.

IAIN GALBRAITH, born in Glasgow in 1956, grew up in the village of Arrochar in the west of Scotland. His poems have appeared in a wide range of journals including *Poetry Review*, *PN Review*, the *Times Literary Supplement*, *New Writing*, *Irish Pages* and *Edinburgh Review*, and his volume of poetry *The True Height of the Ear* was published by Arc in 2018.

His recent translations from German include W. G. Sebald's *Across the Land and the Water. Selected Poems 1964-2001* (Hamish Hamilton, 2011), Jan Wagner's *Self-portrait with a Swarm of Bees* (Arc, 2015), and Esther Kinsky's novel *River* (Fitzcarraldo Editions, 2018).

He has won numerous prizes for his work as a translator, including the Stephen Spender Prize for Poetry Translation (2014), the Popescu Prize for European Poetry Translation (2015), and the Schlegel-Tieck Prize (2017).